MESSENGER WITH A MESSAGE

Gloria Lee Taylor

Published in Nigeria by Rextun Publishing Co

No1, Alimi Road, G.R.A, Ahmadu Bello way

Ilorin. Kwara State - Nigeria.

+2348038876748, 07068357963

ISBN: 9798781700127

DEDICATION

This work is to my children, grandchildren, friends, and Rex, a man who has
become the embodiment of the qualities and principles in this work.
It is also for my family's love, respect, support, and confidence over many years.
Rex, thanks for helping me to understand the gifts and essence of my messages.
To my lovely daughter Tomiko, who I believed when she told me at the age of
sixteen, that i would write a book. She has always encouraged me to write and to
listen to what God is telling me to write.
To my lovely daughters, Alycia and Porscha, with who I have learned the essence
of learning how to be patient and use what I have learnt over the years, put it on
paper so others can read.
To my handsome son, who always tell me to be happy while making me feel special
by telling me how proud he is of me and for me to keep shining.
And to every one of you my friends and partners; thank you for letting me discover
and experience the joy of dignity, equality and the fulfillment that was created in
me. You all have given more than yourself, prayed, and loved me the hardest when
I didn't understand. The nights I cried and you all were with me in some of those
moments. I am so glad God gave me the opportunity to be your mother and best
friends. I want you all to know that this leap of growth has made me love you all
even harder than before.
I pray that I will always be teachable, trainable and a continuous learner, because
the word of God must be taught.

Love you family

CONTENTS

INTRODUCTION

"Wisdom is the principal thing; therefore get wisdom: and with all thy getting
get understanding."
   -Proverbs 4:7

On a Sunday morning, sitting on the second row behind Pastor Taylor as I do every Sunday; the Shout Band, led by my brother-in-law, was really on fire that morning.
 Praises and Worship service was on, and people were crying and shouting. I have always been a quiet person in these sessions, but when I decided to give my life to Christ after being raised in the church, I decided in 2000 to give it a try. I had already done whatever I thought I was grown enough to do.
 So, watching everyone praising him, took me back in reflection to New Orleans, on my daughter's balcony while stationed at the Navy Base. I heard a voice say "you tried love and it failed, try me. Give me a chance and I will love and take care of you."
I remember saying yes to his will. At that moment, I received Christ.
 Running to tell someone how I felt was absolutely awesome. It was the best part of my life. But there always came a time; even as it always was when I was a child; I knew something they were teaching was wrong. But my mother would always say "shh, be quiet, you can't say this". And

everything we did, we were going to hell.

My mother and father had six children; 3 girls, 3 boys, and I am the eldest. I lived only after the seventh miscarriage, weighing only 2lbs.

The doctor gave me a week to live. I've had good times and bad times; but through it all God brought me out. I wanted to teach God word, so much that I could taste it. I taught Bible Study, Sunday School, and planned many events and programs. Then I always wanted to teach anything dealing with helping my people, save and unsaved. God has no respectable person.

We need to stop sleeping and sugar coating the truth to live in a society that hates God's people. We are a people of love and kindness. I believe our ancestors died so that we also should live and not die. This book is to give you something to think about. The discussion I am writing about is interesting to me. So I want to share some with you and hope it makes you think. I don't want to go into a long discussion at the moment, just an introduction of what's to come. From a small child my vision and dreams were to go home to the Motherland; to be a blessing to God's people; my people.

We are his chosen one and the sooner we learn that and stop living the oppressed lifestyle but know that the Bible is about us so we can ask for Wisdom, Knowledge, and Understanding.

This verse explains it all; (2 Chronicles 4:17) says:
"if My people who are called by My name will humble themselves, and pray and seek My face, and turn from their wicked ways, then I will hear from heaven, and forgive their sin and heal their land."

It's all a learning process and we will be learning till we leave this earth. If God's people will teach us to reject our pride, seek after him, and repent and pray, he will definitely listen to us, we must be real and honest with the Father, he is all knowing, all seeing, all powerful, all loving. So let's get ready to read some discussion, some will disagree and some agree and can add more to the discussion. This is a book to make you think about what we know and don't know, the secrets and mysteries of the Bible. We need to get our house in order. Have you been hired by God, there is no application, no references, no work history. When God hires you, you are always in his family of love. Going to Bible College woke me up, to the fact that Christianity was built on controlling God's people. The church thinks that if you don't conform to their rules, regulations you are going to hell. They forgot Jesus said come as you are. So Let's Go!!!!!! And see what Gloria's Moments, all about.

My Recommended Prayer for the People of God

My Prayer is that the word of God will shine everywhere I go.
I come to you God, empty, that you might fill me up. I love having these
conversations with you, my father. I thank you for your love and
forgiveness.
For all thy blessings this morning, when my eyes came open, I have activity
in my limbs; i can hear, speak, put on my clothes, feed myself, and i can
think. God you have been so good to me and I am very grateful.
Thank you for my children, grandchildren, great grand's, the children that
you have placed in my life; my family that you gave me, and the friends;
even for my enemies; I give you thanks father.
Today is the day the Lord has made, I will be glad and rejoice in it.
Whoever needs encouragement, peace, strength, love, joy, God grant them.
Heal their bodies. Grant my enemies the Love they need in order to realize
without you they have nothing. Forgive me when I get so involved with
other things and seem like I am pushing you away. You said in your words,
I can be the head and not the tail.
(Deuteronomy 28:13). Teach me love, so that my light comes before me.
Keep building a fence around me, everyday. Protect me as I travel on my

way. Give me wisdom, knowledge, and understanding of your words.
 Forgive me Jesus, I ask you to present faultless before the father. That he may enlarge my
Territory and keep me safe from all hurt and danger. (1Chronicles 4:10, Psalm 23-The Lord is my Shepherd, and I shall not want, I remember hearing God speak those words to me so powerfully in
2011, that when I say it was God, I knew it was him. (Psalm 1:1) "Blessed is the man," I am blessed, I am who the father, says I am, can do what the fathers says I can do. Thank you God, for letting me know I am a child of the most High God. Let miracles take place in lives, heal homes, marriages, hospitals; go inside prison camps, amidst homeless children, abusive relationships, schools, and whatever I didn't include, I know that you know my heart. God, even those that believe you don't exist, show them who you are that you may get the Glory.
I pray that God gives us peace. I pray that this will be done on earth as in heaven. That we be in obedience to God and never be anxious for anything. I am here to testify that you are a God of many chances. Help us God to be what you will have us to be. I pray for protection and safety for everyone reading this prayer, that today God will touch you and heal and give you comfort and the strength you need to overcome. We need you; I need your restoration, your love and hope in my heart. I trust you Lord that you will heal our broken hearts. Remove everything that causes grief, stress, sorrow in our lives and current situations. Guide us God, make our enemies be at peace with us. Give our leaders wisdom as they try to navigate during this pandemic. We want your power, glory to be on display, so the world will know "King of Kings "do live in us that let him in. Clearly some of us are praying for no more violence, fighting. Please father go before us, you are the present and past, by your hands we are all created in your image. We have no way of knowing what is coming our way. I pray we keep smiling, be grateful, stay strong, work hard, stay humble, be kind, never give up, most of all believe in yourself. God is going to allow us to recover everything you lost.

I know these to be true God, you did it for me, I know you will do it for others. Not my will, but yours Lord.
 In the name of the father, son and Holy Spirit.
Amen!!!!!!!

Chapter 1
Being a Servant of the Most High God

I am a servant of the most High God; I wanted to be a disciple. My ministry is being fulfilled because I was determined to see this all the way.

No one knows how many years I have prayed for this opportunity and feel that God is training me to walk in love, help his flock. The truth is my faith is growing stronger and to have fruits of the spirit is what I want to be seen in my life; not only the spiritual blessings of learning God's words but building on what he says and not what man says.

(Jeremiah 29-11) For I know the plans I have for you, "declares the Lord," plans to prosper you

and not to harm you, plans to give you hope and a future. This is a new journey, walking in love, to learn more about my Savior and teach his words. In the book (Habakkuk 2: 2-3) "The Lord replied" Write the vision, and make it plain upon tables, that he may run that readeth it. For the vision is yet for an appointed time, but at the end it shall speak, and not lie: though it tarry, wait for it; because it will surely come, it will not tarry.

This book gave me an understanding of how close Habakkuk was with God, that he held a conversation with God and he didn't understand why God was passing judgment on the people, when he felt like it was a lost cause.

But when he got so frustrated, he went into prayers and praises. Then he stopped running to begin to do what God called him to do. I wont go into the whole story, but the Prophet encourages believers to wait on the Lord, expecting that he will work out all situations for our good. So I will write it down and make it plain that even an unbeliever will understand that if you wait on it, it shall come to pass.

I am a living witness, and here I am trying to write what I have learnt to share with others willing to stand on God's words.

The Most High is concerned about all these titles in the book of Ephesians 4:11 where the Apostle Paul tells us that Jesus gave us prophets, pastors, evangelists, and teachers. So, He gave us all of these leadership titles, but beyond those titles, Are you a SERVANT?

The Bible says blessed are those servants who the Lord finds watching when he comes. The Lord wants to know who is faithful and wise to place over his household.

In (Exodus 3: 18) Moses was a servant in leading the nation of Israel. I want that; and we all should want the same humility that Moses had even when it came to leadership.

I pray and believe that God will help me to have the characteristics of a good and faithful servant.

- Being faithful
- Being a witness
- Being available
- Helping others
- Showing humility
- Practicing forgiveness
- Participating in Spiritual disciplines ,

 All these qualities are what people of God should have, and we must continue to ask for the grace to possess them; above all, showing love to everyone. In showing these I can have a relationship with the Most High, and know that when I speak it's of God.

Chapter 2
Taught to Pray

As a child I was taught to say my prayers at night, and whenever we are sitting down to eat, no matter where I am.

Over the years it became a life-style. As an adult I taught my children to pray, and it became a conversation piece, before bed. Now my grands and great grands are taught to say their prayers.

We ought to coach our children so that when they get older they know how to reverence God. I love to pray, but when I watch others pray, I feel my prayers are too short or too long. I pray all the time, even when I am walking, riding, it doesn't matter. The Bible says pray without ceasing meaning pray repeatedly and as often as you can and want.

I have seen people pray for hours, and some pray for entertainment, just for someone to comment he //she can really pray. Wow!!!!

But when we really want an answer from God, we need to have a conversation with Him. A heart to heart conversation with sincerity of heart and most importantly, pray according to His will.

In my prayer life, i talk to him just like I talk to you. I build a relationship with him; even if He doesn't answer me right then I keep going every day. You can't give up. He's your father, he never sleep nor slumber.

Jesus told us, "When you pray, do not pray as the hypocrites, for they love to pray standing in the synagogues and street corners, to be seen by men. But when you pray, go into your room, close your door, and pray to the Most High who hears everything.

(Matthew 6:9-13, and Luke 11:2-4) In these prayers God is acknowledged to be directing and giving us a clear meaning to everything. Let God's will and his purpose show through everything; that's the power of God.

A prayer to me is just like worship; you get the chance to build a relationship with Him. God loves building a relationship, remember He is the bridegroom and the church is His bride. When you ask God for things and it manifests at the right time then you are on the right level. Prayer makes you feel that the Almighty is listening because you are sincere about what you are asking in your heart. To ask, seek, and knock for the doors to be open unto you; you need to pray to be a blessing not only to yourself but to others as well.

Some of us are still here because of the prayers of our grandparents, parents, or because somebody somewhere in the world was praying for me, you and others. We may never meet them, but God answers their prayers concerning you and me.

 In 2000 when I gave my life back to Christ, I was proud to go into Pastor's study and pray for her, and sometimes whoever asks.

 Just being in the presence of the Woman of God or the Man of God, and to pray for and with them is honor to me. One thing I know is God adds no sorrow.

Praying like someone else is not being truthful to God, or yourself. Come to God, as you are, just open your mouth and the words will come.

After writing this I truly realize that I don't have to pray long, just speak what God places in you and without trying to be so eloquent and long. Now if that's your style, I have no problem. Different styles for everyone. All God is concerned about is your heart and if it's in the right place when you pray.

Learning to pray comes with struggles, pain, but I'm trusting God and knowing that he will bring you out.

 I am a disciple, God said he will never leave me or forsake me. So I pray that the God inside me is used to help others, to keep them lifted up in prayers. To always walk in his words, his promise, and know without a shadow or doubt that he will do just what you ask. Even when we don't know how to pray, Jesus intercedes for us before the father.

God said he will renew your mind and he does. Pray to God in secret and he will reward you openly.

Are you teaching your children to pray? (Proverbs 4:20-22) My child pay attention to what I say. Listen carefully to my words. Don't lose sight of them, let them penetrate deep into your heart, for they bring life to those who find them, and healing to their whole body. May our children harken to our words as we teach them the way to the father. Amen.

Chapter 3
Baptism in the Holy Spirit

Baptism in the Holy Spirit is not used for the development of holiness in the individual. It is an empowerment for service. We were told in the New Testament that a comforter would come.

Jesus told the disciples not to leave Jerusalem; but to wait on the gift that the father promised.

John baptized with water; and in few days the converts will be baptized in the Holy Spirit (Acts 1:4-5). All these demonstrate that the baptism of the Holy Spirit is not what cleanses us. It empowers the saved for service in the vineyard of the father.

Jesus said when the Holy Spirit comes on you; the disciples will be his witnesses in Jerusalem, and all of Judea, Samaria, to the ends of the earth. Their names were already written in the book; so are our names written in the book. We are clean before God, having a spiritual bath through Christ word (John 13:10; 15:3). We today don't realize we all need a Spiritual Bath, every once in a while to reconnect with the father.

Sometimes when praying, worshiping, or whatever you do isn't working, then do something out of the ordering. The Bible speaks about foolish things (1Corinthians 1:27). The baptism of the spirit is not something given to us for our glory and honor, but to enable us to do God's will. So water baptism is the symbol of my surrender to God, indicating that I am willing to do his will and live by his standards. Baptism of the Spirit put simply, is the work of the Holy Spirit in the life of the one fully surrendered to God. Water baptism is a once in a lifetime experience.

Frequently asked Questions about baptism:
(1) I got baptized and made a mistake, do I get re-baptized?

(2) I'm already a Christian, but join another church, do I need to get re-baptized at the other church?

(3) The difference between dedication and baptism?

(4) What is the difference between water and Holy Spirit baptism?

In (Acts 1:5) Jesus said in a few days you will be baptized with the Holy Spirit. John immersed you in water; I am going to cleanse you in the Holy Spirit. This is what we need in order to be effective instruments of our lord in the world.

Filled with the Spirit

So when the baptism with the Spirit comes, it is like a mighty wind immersing and filling all the house with a sound.

The Prophet Joel said: "And in the last days it shall be, (God declares) , that I will pour out my Spirit upon all flesh and your Sons and your Daughters shall prophesy;

Jesus didn't say, "wait in Jerusalem until you are born again or converted or put into the body of Christ." He says, "Wait until you are fully clothed with power." He didn't say, "you shall receive membership in the body of Christ when the Holy Spirit has come upon you, " he says," you shall receive power when the Holy Spirit has come upon you.

History of Baptism of Holy Spirit

In (Acts 6) we meet Stephen who is full of faith and the Holy Spirit. Verse eight, speaks of him that he was therefore full of power and did wonders and signs among the people. But specifically in verse ten, the leaders could not resist the wisdom and spirit with which he spoke. His fullness with Holy Spirit gave him extraordinary power for the Christ-Exalting Ministry.

 In (Acts 9:17) Paul is filled with the Holy Spirit at his conversion and the result was that he spoke with such extraordinary power that the Jews of Damascus were confounded (Acts 9:22). In (Acts 11:24) Barnabas was full of the Holy Spirit and faith and the effect Luke mentioned was that "A large company was added to the Lord" (At Pentecost).

 In (Acts 13:9) Paul was filled with the Holy Spirit as he spoke to Elymas the magician and God gave him the power to pronounce Elymas blind for a season (Acts 13:11).

Conclusions:

Luke says being baptized in the spirit is being clothed with power from on high so the message of Christ can be taken effectively to all the nations of the world (Luke 24:49). Therefore in the Christian churches, the sprinkling of water onto a person's forehead, or putting them into water, symbolizes purification or regeneration most of all in the church.

Chapter 4
What Is Worship?

Worship is to show lots of love and adoration for something. Worship is an extreme form of love and unconditional devotion. If you spend time with God then you love God.

 If we are truly sold out to God, do we question him or trust him and never ask questions? What would your answer be to this?

The dictionary says worship is a feeling or expression, or shows of reverence and adoration for; honor with religious rites.

When I first came to Christ, it was the most beautiful part in my life of salvation. There were songs, hymns, even scriptures that touched my heart and I would just talk to God, as if he was there in front of me.

That's the spiritual awakening I had and still have with the father. Worship is like a transformation in

Which I feel God takes me on a journey of outer body experience. Worship is not about me, it's how I show love, giving God all of me; and in praise with thanksgiving,   we cry, we dance; fall out under the unction of the Holy Spirit. We must worship God by glorifying him in his presence with our hearts, voices, and beliefs. The more we /I get to know God the more we can worship him for all he has done for us.

 I always owe him praise; worship him in truth and spirit. In the past days, I loved slow music and still do. Coming to Christ gave me a new dance, as

David did. Just listening to worship songs, and the way it just fills me up; the tears, and my thoughts of where God has brought me from, I know I owe him worship. This song means so much to me:

"Sanctuary", God prepares me, as living sacrifice, holy and acceptable to him, is my worship.

On Sunday's I love to sing that song.

Sometimes the things we do and have done in life cause us to ask God for forgiveness, but we ought to remember we are all a part of God's body. In church sometimes , watching someone worship God and the songs they sing, takes you into absolutely deep part of your soul, and the overflow of his words that's inside of you begin to make you call on him , tell him your request and thank him for what he's already doing and the things you don't know about. So please remember all religions have different ways to worship.

Build a close relationship with God, and let him know that you worship him in spirit and in truth. (Psalm 46:9) " O worship the Lord in the beauty of holiness: fear before him, all the earth". So remember, worship is who God is in your life and how you express yourself. Worship is praising God, and waiting on a response, which he is always on time to give.

I am not worshiping God because I was taught as a child, but because of the love he has for me. Even when I feel I am not worthy he lets me know I am not perfect, but I am his child worthy of his love. "I love you God"!!!!!!

Intimacy: my Closeness with the Father

My thoughts on Worship are that spiritual intimacy is the best feeling in the world; a well being, and loving how special I feel just knowing he gave his life for me that I can be who the Father has called me to be. My relationship with God creates a purpose.

When the Shout Band plays, it was my time to praise God, and it made me dance the more. When I glorify God, I believe I worship God from my heart; it was me emptying myself out to him and asking him to forgive me for my sins. I also want him to know that I am thankful, and grateful for all the things he has done for me, and doing at the moment.

The people of God are to remember God's deeds of salvation. The attitude we come with determines our worship. Over the years I have learnt that Biblical worship involves numerous signs and symbols. They are all around us everyday.

Everything God has created gives worship and praises to Him. Even the trees, mountains, water gives God reverence. When I was a child we would sing a song, "If the robin can give praise, why can't we?

Have you ever noticed birds singing and pecking early in the morning, giving thanks? The rooster crows for another day. Worship does change your life as you begin a relationship with God. Worship means to bow down or to prostrate oneself before God. Everyone is a worshipper, I love to worship, it makes me feel as if I am slow dancing with the Father.

I have placed things before God. Social media, and other things, I had to repent; nothing should come before the Father. Sometimes I have to remember I am serving a jealous God. And anything we put ahead of him is a sin. We all fall short.

"Thou shalt have no other gods before me". (Exodus 20: 3-5 and Deuteronomy 5:7-8). We all have a way of worshiping God, just like our hearts beat differently; he knows our hearts when they are sincere about whatever we are talking to God about. He listens and answers prayers. Worship therefore is intimacy with the creator, who searches the heart, and knows what the mind of the spirit is.

The Holy Spirit intercedes for me and the saints according to the will of God. So when I am worshiping God, I feel he is talking to me at that moment, where I am totally into him, even at home resting in his arms as I hear his soft voice.

God talks to us when we as individuals know his voice. He might not talk to me in the same way He talks to you. Because (Hebrews 5:13-14) explains that: Anyone who has to drink milk is still a baby without experience in the word of God.

But when you get older you can eat solid food as a mature person for yourself and those in leadership that have been trained to distinguish good and evil. As you meditate you can go into worship; Knowing that worship is a close contact to God.

I tried to introduce worship during Bible Studies by introducing the different styles of worship and no one was interested because, sometimes people love praises more than worship.

I learnt over the years, there are different cultures of praise. So when you are taught praise is worship, you let God handle that.

I was raised in church, and we went to church so much that I decided that when I become an adult, I won't go to church for a long time. I ran for a long time.

Now however, my intimacy with God is so sweet that I love being in His presence and also talking about him; His goodness; and how he lets me know that I am special.

I learnt that worship shows in our lives and shapes our behaviors.

Everyone has a different experience when worshiping God. Listen to his voice and you can feel the energy of the spirit- having encounters with the Father.

Being a person that loves trees, I considered myself a tree with beautiful

branches, beautiful leaves, and roots. This symbolizes all the lives I am going to touch. My vision was clear as day. That there will be lives touched everyday in a form of worship to help someone transform into his likeness.
 We as the church have gotten away from the intimacy of having personal experiences with God, and church has become more entertaining and controlling than the real worship.
 When we are having intimacy with the Holy Spirit, we don't have the time to be jealous of another person's praise or worship.
Songs make you move, and your spirit gets connected to sounds of the drums and all the instruments to make joyful noises unto the Lord. Psalm has a way of feeding your spirit, which can make you worship in a dance. David danced before the Lord (2 Samuel 6:14) that was worship.
Above all, once you receive Jesus you become part of the family and whether you are involved in worship, praises or intercession, it is all directed by God.
 Always remember prayer begins with worship. To worship God is to acknowledge His worth and give Him honor and reverence. When we love God and trust Him in all we do, we acknowledge His worth, who He is and what He has done for us, and will do in our lives. I therefore worship Him because He has become my (Elohim) creator, (El Shaddai) the all - sufficient one, (Jehovah-Jireh) the lord will provide, (Adonai) Lord,Master, (Jehovah-Nissi); the Lord is my Banner, (Jehovah-Raah) the lord is my shepherd, (Jehovah-Rapha) the lord who heals.
These are just a few names that stood out in my situation. All God's names are important, but these are about my relationship with the Father and why I believe that my intimacy with him is so important to me.
This is spiritual, and when it becomes physical, I remind myself of (Genesis 6:3) "My spirit shall not always strive with man, for that he also is flesh: yet his days shall be a hundred and twenty years."

Time to Pray
"Father, I come to thank you and to spend time with you today.
Worshiping you has been a
Pleasure; thinking of all your love, and just holding a conversation with you about me and what you mean to me.
I thank you Father for whoever is reading this, grant them their heart's desire, give them strength, humbleness, meekness, self-control, happiness, joy, peace, love, and patience.
 I pray for my loved ones, even my enemies. Help me to be a blessing to your people, keep
us safe from all hurt, harm and danger.

Thank you for making a way when it seem all else has failed.

Also thank you for opening my eyes to see the truth, and my ears that I may hear what the spirit is saying.

I believe Jesus is your Son, and he died so that I might have the right to the tree of life. I am praying that I be sensitive to the spirit. God we are willing, I am willing to do your will now while the entire world lies in the power of the evil one. I present myself as a living sacrifice. Your will is our will God, good, acceptable, perfect, we love you and we have no doubts about your love for us.

God bless the homeless people, those in hospitals, rest homes, prison camps.

You know what everyone needs and want more than I do. Bless people on their jobs and those searching for a job. Feed the hungry people, and the animals. We need you Father to come and see us.

We are in need of restoration and regeneration. God search my heart and see if there's any hurtful ways, pains in me and if I am walking in agreement with you. God bless those who are rulers over us, and protect us all over the world. Leave no one out God. You made us all, and you are sitting high and looking low. Put your hedge around your people in every part of the world. Heal the land far and near.

I am asking and knocking, seeking you God. I am pleading that you will come and see about us all, we are in need of hearing from you God. I know you have a specific plan for each of our lives and specific work for each of us to do.

You have the power and the glory, forever and ever.

Forgive me Father, and wash me clean. Thank you for listening to me. In the name of the Father;

Son; Holy Spirit.

Amen

Discussion Questions:
•   Who will enter the Kingdom of Heaven?

....

....

....

....

....

....

....

....

- Whom does God hear, and why?

....

....

....

....

....

....

....

....

- What is submission?

....

....

....

....

....

....

....

....

- Why did Jesus Pray?

....

....

....

....

....

....

....

- Why did Paul want them to be filled with the knowledge of God's will?

....

....

....

....

....

....

....

- What would keep you from knowing God?

. . . .
. . . .
. . . .
. . . .
. . . .
. . . .
. . . .
. . . .

- In what areas of your life do you need directions?

. . . .
. . . .
. . . .
. . . .
. . . .
. . . .
. . . .

- Look at what God tells us about Jesus Christ. Read (Hebrews 4:14) and write what this verse
tells you about him.

. . . .
. . . .
. . . .
. . . .
. . . .
. . . .
. . . .
. . . .

- Does the situation described in Isaiah 59 sound similar to today? To our culture? What was needed?

. . . .
. . . .
. . . .
. . . .
. . . .
. . . .
. . . .

- Did you know that (Isaiah 53 is one of the clearest Old Testament prophecies about the Christ? Look at what Isaiah told us prophetically about Jesus in (Isaiah 53:12. Take notes of what he did and whom he intercedes and write your observation.

....
....
....
....
....
....
....
....
....
....
....
....
....
....
....

•	Read (Revelation 1:5-6) what do you see in these verses that place you in a beautiful intercession?

....
....
....
....
....
....
....

•	Why don't you sit quietly before the Lord and ask him to lay a specific person on your heart and mind ? Ask God how to pray for this person, to lead you in prayer on his or her behalf.

....
....
....
....
....
....
....

•	Read (Hebrews 11:2) In one word, how did men gain approval?

....
....
....
....

....
....
....
....

- Read (James 4:4) what is the problem there?

....
....
....
....
....
....
....
....

- Explain (Psalm 23) in your own words.

....
....
....
....
....
....
....
....

- How would you explain to a sinner, what being saved means?

....
....
....
....
....
....
....
....

- Has God ever disciplined you?

....
....
....
....
....
....
....
....

- In (Colossians 3:12-13) is a passage on forgiveness gives us an example of what we are forgiving. What is it?

....
....
....
....
....
....
....

- What is God's word to you?

....
....
....
....
....
....
....

- Why do we need to confess our sins?

....
....
....
....
....
....
....

- What does it mean to ask according to the will of God? Does knowing His word help understand His will?

....
....
....
....
....
....
....

- Read the parables in (Luke 18) how often are we to "ask"?

....
....
....

....
....
....
....
....

Chapter 5
Gift of Tongues

I don't believe you have to speak in tongues as some leaders have stated.
Have I ever spoken in tongues? Some say I have, I don't recall.
The Bible says: For anyone who speaks in a tongue does not speak to men but to God. He who speaks in tongues edifies himself, but he who prophesies edifies the church. I would like every one of you to speak in tongues, but I would rather you have prophecy (1Corinthians 14:1-46).
 I have seen Pastors tell new members to speak in tongues, right after they confess their sins, accept Jesus Christ and gotten saved. I am not saying it cannot happen, but from my point of view I believe that when God is ready he will cause it to happen. Some say the Holy Spirit falls on you as soon as you accept Christ. I am not convinced of that.
Is it Biblical to speak in Tongues?
The New Testament describes tongues as speech addressed to God, but also as something
that can potentially be interpreted into human language, "edifying the hearers" (1Cor.14:5-13).

At Pentecost the speakers were praising God (Acts 2:11;10:46). In (Acts 2:11) talks about
Jesus and converts to Judaism); The Holy Spirit had come down upon the Apostles, and the crowd heard them speak in their own natural dialects. When the Holy Spirit comes, He not only establishes his presence in an individual permanently, but also equip them to spread the news about Jesus forgiving sins and reconverts sinners to God
What happens when we speak in tongues?
Speaking in tongues is a conscious choice, so it makes me know that maybe I quench the fire of the Spirit. Sometimes God needs us to refer back to what is buried deep inside of us. But we must allow the Holy Spirit to manifest himself through the word. When he speaks through me, you'll hear the words but will not understand what I am saying. I have experienced this.
Speaking in tongues builds you up and it is as well a sign for non-believers. Seeing how some churches don't understand this verse baffles me a lot. (1Cor.14:27-28) says if anyone speaks in a tongue, let there be only two or three, and each in turn; let someone interpret. But if there is no one to interpret, let each of them keep silent in church and speak to himself and God.
Now there are some who disobey this law. In (Acts 2:4) A familiar verse, And they were filled with the Holy Spirit and began to speak in other tongues as the scripture gave them utterance.
I believe they were telling the people what God was saying just in the language people could understand. Some years ago, in church I witness seeing this done, if they still do it, I don't know, but the bible says (Mark 16:17) And these signs will accompany those who believes. In my name they will cast out demons, they will speak in tongues, but if you don't speak in tongues then you don't have the Holy Spirit. I don't believe that. I know that God saved me, and I know his voice. We have a relationship, a strong foundation, not built on sinking sand.
He leads and guides me, directing my path. He has brought me out of situations that I know can only be done by God.
This scripture seems so real to me as well, (1Cor.14:29).
Nevertheless in church, I would rather speak five words with my mind in order to instruct others, than ten thousand words in tongue. This is because when unbelievers don't understand what you are speaking in tongues, you just let a soul walk away when you could have spoken from your mind and God will give you what to say.
There are lots of Scriptures that talk about speaking in tongues, and I can't write them all, but the ones that have meanings in my heart and what I stand on, I will testify about them knowing they are truth.

Now what do we think and feel when a false Prophet comes in and speak in tongues and everyone feels he's telling the truth, but you never see any evidence of prophecy. When a man or woman of God, speakers in tongue, interpret it, and you know and truly know without a shadow of doubt and can stand on the word then it's to edifying the church.

God gives us signs in parts. In my understanding:

(1) Do we all possess gifts of healing?

(2) Do we speak or interpret?

(3) Do we all speak with tongues?

Another thing I know is that we can all take our time to give different opinions, but in (1 Cor.12:28) the scripture says, And God has appointed in the church first Apostles, Prophets, Teachers, then Miracles workers, then Gifts of healing, helping, administrating, and various kinds of tongues.

This is my belief as well (Isaiah 28:11) For with stammering lips and another tongue will he speak to his people. Meaning with people of strange lips and foreign tongue God will speak to his people. How will God's words travel if we don't speak in other tongues? The last quoted scripture tells it all.

There are so many more, but to me (1 Cor.14:21-22) says, in the law it is written, "By people of strange tongues and by the lips of foreigners they will speak to their people and even then they will not listen to me, says the Lord". These tongues are a sign, not for believers, but for unbelievers, while prophecy is a sign not for unbelievers but for believers.

The Scriptures teaches us that tongues are genuine languages.

(1) They are not meaningless sounds. So when you speak in tongue and you find yourself repeating the same sounds over and over again, it might indicate you are not speaking in tongue.

(2) We learn from the scriptures that it's the Holy Spirit who enables us to speak in new and unlearned languages (Acts 2:4). We don't invent the language, and we don't invent the "sounds" we speak.

(3) When Speaking in tongues, your mind is unproductive, meaning our mind is not involved in the speaking process. Speaking in tongues is not something we have to think about. The language of the spirit is not connected to the mind, but rather the spirit of man. Mind is not the source of the tongue. If you find yourself having to think about what sounds you will speak next, that is a good indication you are not speaking in tongues. It is spiritually beneficial and best to recognize this and seek the experience than to persist in a false belief and experience, mistaking it for the truth.

Chapter 6
Shepherd

What does the Metaphor of the Shepherd in the Bible mean to you?
A Shepherd is a person who tends and rears sheep. A Shepherd in the Bible is someone who watches over, looks after, or guides somebody. A Shepherd role is responsibility to the safety and welfare of the flock; Keeping a watchful eye on them from the wolf and poisonous plants. The sheep recognize the voice of the Shepherd. They follow him/her. The shepherd gives his life for them.
First I will start with my favorite verse, (Psalm 23:1-6).
One day sitting on the couch, while talking to my daughter, I opened my mouth and all of a sudden "The Lord Is My Shepherd, and I Shall Not Want", just rolled off my tongue, and I heard it; my mouth was moving but it wasn't my voice. It sounds strange, but it's true. God will speak through

you. The 23rd Psalm has meant a lot to me since that day more than ever. God is my shepherd, he feeds me, leads me, clothes me, puts a roof over my head.

The shepherd just as he leads he feeds his flocks. Thy"rod and staff" also tell me God is my shepherd, my leader. It has inspired me to know that God loves me and I shall not want. The meaning of (John 3:16)

For God so loved the world, that he gave his only begotten Son. He loves me just that much; this is very personal to me. Back to (Psalm 23) God's power to guide us, also says fear no evil, powerful reminder of his goodness. I can walk and not fear, he said "yea, though I walk through the valley of the shadow of death, he is with me. His rod and staff will comfort me.

Then he said he will prepare a table before me in the presence of my enemies. And he will anoint my head with oil. My cup runneth over. But surely goodness and mercy shall follow me all the days of my life, this is what the good shepherd said about me, you. He will protect me. The more I seek the Shepherd, the more I can find his love, because he will sustain me, you, and us.

The bible says the sheep recognize the voice of the shepherd, if you have a relationship with the Father, you should know his voice without doubt. In the book of (Isaiah 65:24) we read that: And it shall come to pass that before they call, I will answer; and while they are still speaking, I will hear. The Shepherd will never leave nor forsake you as long as the relationship is in God's grace.

In the gospel of (John 10:11-14) the scripture says "I am the good shepherd" the good shepherd lays down his life for the sheep. Anyone who is hired by the shepherd will run and leave the sheep when the wolf appears, but the Shepherd will always defend his flock.

When I think about leadership I always read (John 10:1-4) the best example of a Shepherd leading his flock to God.

We as sheep follow the shepherd, as the Shepherd leads us we should never run to follow a stranger; but sometimes we stray from the Shepherd, and hit all kinds of detours, wrong turn; U-turns, dead and ends. The road is long and so when we take off to follow the stranger, God still waits on us to return. You have free will, he is a gentleman, never leaves you, he just wants you to turn from your wicked ways, and come back to your first love.

We must also remember the Father has other sheep that are not of this fold. They too listen to his voice. They know the Father's voice just as the Father knows me and you. No one can snatch you from him.

Jesus is the good shepherd because He is God. In (Matthew 20:7) Jesus talks about laborers being hired at different times of the day.

HAVE YOU BEEN HIRED BY GOD?

Chapter 7
The Bible and Science

What can we learn about God from Creation?
We can learn that the power of God is so awesome. (Psalm 24) The earth is the Lord's and the fullness thereof; the world, and they that dwell therein. For he hath founded it upon the seas, and established it upon the floods. Creation also tells us that God as the master shaper of the world is the God of wisdom. When you look at the trees, how big and tall they are, some look as if they're in the clouds; they have been around for years; they experience different seasons and still know exactly when their season is upon them. Awesomeness!

xxx

The mountains hold different resources and plants; animals and fossils are evidences of ancient wisdom.

God takes care of everything He created. He gives the birds, fishes, animals, food and shelter, water and everything they need even to humans he does the same.

 Everything has its own time. Take a look around to see all the beautiful designs, the perfect blueprint; God's position as creator and owner of all gives him the right to make the rules.

In (Colossians 2) the scripture says: For by him (the Son) were all things created, that are in heaven, and that are in earth, visible and invisible.

(Psalm 8:1-9) tells us O Lord our Lord, how Excellent is thy name in all the earth!

Chapter 8
"I can't believe that God plays dice with the Universe."

What are my Thoughts?

I remember reading an article about Albert Einstein, who wrote a personal opinion in a letter which became famous. My thoughts are that Einstein was right, ("God does not play dice.") God's presence is and was all around us and nature and the universe in all its aspects and expressions.

I remember again years ago in a Bible Study someone said God is not the one who causes chaos in the world. So I agree with Einstein, the goal of a scientist should be to begin understanding the universe.

 Einstein had a feeling that nature and the universe and God's nature are the angels that will lead us through all the troubles of life with consultations, strength and uncompromising problems.

But if Quantum Physics is such a useful theory, why did he disagree? Because nothing are certain according to Quantum Physics; and we can only predict how probable an event is to happen.

To me sounds more like a prophecy which God only gives to us in parts. As Einstein believed, how you can predict a six to come out when you throw dice. But we have played games and tried to predict the outcome. That's why he disagreed, because every physical properties of each individual particle can, and must be measured with high precision. Quantum Physics does not allow that, it tells us about how probable it is for system or particles to behave in a certain way, but it will never tell us about how each individual particle will behave. That's why he believes "God does not play dice". I agree nothing is coincidental. What happened was already predestined and what will happen is already decided. That's what he meant: We know God, don't gamble, especially with people's lives. Everyone is precious to him.

(2 Peter 3:9) tells us about his love for us. God is not slow, He is patient with us, because He does not desire anyone to be lost, but He desires repentance.

Einstein hated quantum, because it is a theory of probabilities. My thoughts also are that even though people thought Einstein was an atheist, he was using "God" as a Metaphor. He believed in mathematical laws of nature, so his idea of God was someone who formulated the laws and then left the universe alone.

Quantum Mechanics says there is a world of tiny particles behind everything.

On January 3rd 1954, a letter was written saying "The word God is for me nothing more than the expression and product of human weakness; the Bible, a collection of honorable, but still primitive legends...For me other Jewish religion like all other religions is an incarnation of the most childish superstitions." That was Einstein's message.

My own thoughts are that we are where we are as a result of our past actions, and decisions. Change one decision or action and we will be somewhere else. Although he "didn't believe in (free will). He did believe in the principle of causality, not only in physics but including all human actions. I agree with the facts that there's a world of tiny particles behind everything that is joined by complete randomness since he didn't accept Quantum Mechanics, which he denied till his death.

He was wrong but he believed that everything in the universe was driven by hard, deterministic chains of cause and effect. He saw the hand of God in precisely the nature of physical laws, in their mathematical beauty and elegance, in their simplicity. To me there was the fact that natural laws the human mind could discover was evidence of a God; not a God who supersede these laws but one who created them.

He felt that natural law can not be like dice. God isn't one who takes on chance or luck. His creation and the existence itself have a meaning. Einstein got that and so he came up with his phrase, meaning "All what exist has a reason and is a part of a master plan". Nothing is by chance, everything is by design. Einstein didn't like randomness; he thought things were more "determined" than that. He also realized "The more I study science, the more I believe in God". In other words, God's creation was international, and its structure, masterful.

God does not do anything random. There is an order and system in everything if you observe nature.

Chapter 9
Creation

The Wonderful Unscientific Teaching of Christianity
It has been an interesting historical point that the contemporary creation movement began not in the pulpit but in the laboratory. I have learned that creationists have definite scientific and biblical reasons for holding their

position. Creation movement began where scientists, trained to understand and evaluate this physical world, to see clear evidence of the hand of God. Not all scientists were Christians. This evidence, they would argue supports rather than contradicts biblical accounts and claims of creation. Many theologians have decided that claims made by the majority of scientists represent scientific "facts". These facts represent ultimate truth, which must be understood in biblical teaching. However, the Bible contains many claims and events that want to be accepted as "scientific." Are these claims now unacceptable to Christians?

The Scripture record occurrences of many miracles performed by God. In the dictionary a miracle is an event not explainable by natural processes. Are these miracles going to be accepted as "scientific"? What do these theologies propose we do biblical miracles? In (Luke 8:22-25), when Jesus calm the sea, it says it was immediate and complete.

Disciples knew they had just witnessed a supernatural, rather than a natural event. From my research "if Jesus spoke and an hour later the storm gradually dispersed and the waves gradually subsided, the result would have been the same -calm of the sea, but from a human perspective there would be a dramatic difference. No longer would his disciples view the event as miraculous. They would have related it to natural weather patterns. Time will make the event more "scientifically acceptable", as express time can turn a miracle demonstrating Christ's authority over nature into a natural phenomenon."

In the same manner, time also gives the perception of turning God's miracle of creation into a strictly natural phenomenon. No one will ever argue that natural forces could form the stars and planets, let alone life, in just six days. In the minds of some people, given enough time the natural formation of the universe (including life) not only becomes more likely , but almost inevitable. While we strongly challenge the scientific validity of such a position, for those people time will soon sufficiently remove God the creator that he can be replaced with Nature as the creator.

The Resurrection and Science

The Gospel proclaims that Jesus arose from the dead. The resurrection is the core principle of Christianity. Paul declared if Jesus didn't really rise from the dead, then Christianity has nothing to offer (1Corinthians 15:18-20). The Bible claims that all those who are in Christ will be resurrected as well (1Thessalonians 4:16). This last belief about those in Christ is even more unscientific than resurrection from the dead.

Scientific fact is that bodies of dead people do not come back to life. Christianity is built on what could be called a very unscientific claim; the Resurrection.

The power of Christianity is not in becoming more palatable to the scientific community. The power of Christianity (and its ability to reach not just the scientific community but everyone) is the person of Christ and his living word. It's the power to change the human heart. Attempting to make Christianity conform or fit with human knowledge (the opinion of some scientists) does not give it more power or authority.

Science is empowered by understanding how it provides insight into God's creation. Johann

Kepler, 17th century astronomer is credited with saying he studied and understood the cosmos, Johann Kepler, also indicated that scientific research,God's thoughts after Him." He also believed that scientists must guard against the propensity to "glorify our own minds instead of giving God the glory. Science use for the glory of God can be a powerful tool of human understanding. When Science gives testimony of the creator; the people often grow in the biblical understanding and spiritual maturity. It is a situation that theologians should desire.

The Image of God

How does it impact me as a Christian?

I love the fact that whatever you read about the image of God consists of both a natural and moral image, not a physical one. We were made from the dust of the earth. When God formed man, he gave him everything he needed to enjoy his creation, and he also gave us the mind to think for ourselves.

There is a need of us Christian to know the difference between:

(1) The Natural Man

(Ephesians 2:1-2) we are dead in our transgressions and sins, which we live and followed the ways of this world and the ruler of the Kingdom of the air, the spirit who is now at work in those of us who is disobedient . But this person who is not a Christian can't understand and can't accept these thoughts from God, which the Holy Spirit teaches us.

(2) The Spiritual Man

Has his insight into everything and that bothers the Man of the world, who can't understand him at all. (1 Corinthians 2:15) as we learn about the Image of God, we know the mind of a sinful man is death, but our mind controlled by the spirit is life and peace.

To say humans are in the image of God we first must recognize the special qualities of human nature which allows God to be made manifest in our human lives. When God made us in his image, he reached way down in the soil and made us nothing but the best.

So since we are made in his image we are guided by direct spiritual access to him.

As a Christian it makes me want to know more about teaching his words to everyone in my life and family. It impacts me as where I set my mind on things above, not on earthly things which leads to sin.

I try keeping my heart in the right place; to love everyone, even my enemies. The image of God is what I want others to see in my life. When I am dead "I want my family and friends, even my enemies, to say she always did her best at showing love and teaching. God, want you to give your flower while you are alive, because when dead, I can't see or smell them. But while I am alive I can hear the word of God. As a Christian we are told those with ears let them hear every person, age, ethnicity, language, and occupation.

To live but not exist

During the trend in the past-civil war, Southern literature was based on the war between citizens of the same country; dealing with issues of racial and social identity in the past-civil war. South deromanticizing , was a word used to remove the romantic ideas, or heroic aura.

To "live but not exist" was a way of doing things to cope with life. We have dreams, visions, but to exist we must be positive. Speak things as though they were. There are ways to live and not exist. I have fears and try to remember, God didn't give us fear but spirit of sound mind. So I am learning how to shine and associate with light-minded people, that encourages me.

When my Mother died with Alzheimer and Dementia, my Father had a stroke twice to the brain. My world fell apart to watch them both die in my arms. No one can prepare you for that. I stopped living for myself, but then I had to pull myself together, for my children. It was challenging knowing that some family members wanted to place her in a retirement home; this was in spite of them being parents that raised six children! Not on my watch. The thought really shocked me.

And I recalled one night out of nowhere, I stood up to testify and my mouth said, when my parents gets to a point where they need help, I will do it. Where that came from I don't know, but I was built for the test and yes, it was hard.

Then God strengthened me to take care of them. And to see the others take the Estate was like you waiting on them to die and not share with me, was hurtful. But I am living and not existing and never asking for anything because I know God is a provider.

I went to church one Sunday and the Pastor preached on (Matthew 6:25-34) and it blessed me to the point that I knew God has my back. So I don't have to just exist, but I can live cause just existing I would have given up so many times.

It is an experience that I chose to share because whatever we face; issues with family, friends, or anyone; we can live, not exist.

Zombies exist because they are just here and some of us are like Zombies, Sleepwalking through life. I don't want to be a sleepwalker, I choose to live and enjoy life.

 (Genesis 28:6-22) tells us we can be awake but sleeping. You can be physically awake but spiritually asleep. We must not live in the past. It's however good to remember the past and build on it.

 When you exist and not living "The Bible says, 'He who loves sleep and the folding of the hands, poverty will set upon you like a thief in the night. This is because" We are spiritually sleepwalking; existing in a world of our own.

 (1Thessalonians 5:6-16) says, let's not exist through life like those others. Let's keep our eyes open and be smart. Don't waste your days trying to prolong them. I shall use my time. The proper function of man is to live and not to exist.

"A New Beginning"

 I am living!!!!! For the last four years I just existed. But God proved to me he is faithful and answer prayers. If I die, I can say thank you God, for He gave me a new life, a new chance; such that when I look back over my life, I know that i am living.

Jesus came that we might have life and more abundantly, freedom to live not exist.

But in all, I am living my best life and it feels great. I can do all things through Christ. So to live but not exist is just a state of the mind. Dreams and Visions do come true, prayers help.

I thank God that I am living and not existing, I live my dream. Living and waking up every morning is a blessing. Playing with my grandchildren and great-grands, family members, giving makes me happy moments of living not sleepwalking and acting like a zombie.

 Learn to do as much as possible through meditation, but also through bringing your focus back to the present as much as you can in everything you do.

Live!!!!!

My Conclusion

Today I come to you to tell you about a Man that was born to take on my sins and your sins. And that man Jesus Christ, didn't have to do it but he did. You or I can't really imagine the agony He took for you and me to live and not die; to live and not exist. What a price to pay for us as disobedient children of God, who loves us so much he sent a Savior. How many of you will give your lives? How many of you are willing to tell the story about a man that loves you despite your shortcomings?
My Topic- Blood of Christ

Negative Side

B- The boldness I had to do just about whatever I wanted and thought was right.
L- The loneliness I felt, the love I had for the wrong person and the things I felt made me happy. Lust   always creeps in when you least expect.
O-offers I took, knowing they were wrong. Offended by something I could have overlooked. But I knew and thought I was able to handle it when I was just a little church girl. They called me, because I wanted the experience of the wild side.
 O- Oppression that took place when I didn't know which way to go. The bad relationship I placed myself in, when I knew it was wrong. But to be loved sometimes we play victim or become the victim.
 D- Death was knocking at my door; because I had to learn myself. And figure out if you want to keep living in sin or change. My Positive Side So the Blood of Christ - refers in Theology- the physical blood actually shed by Jesus Christ on the cross, and the salvation which Christianity teaches was accomplished clearly and the sacrament blood present in the Lord's Supper. I know that when I came into Christ asked for his forgiveness and accepted him as my Savior, his Blood became my deliverer.

 B- Change into New Beginning of a new journey of a different lifestyle.
 L- Change into love, live, laugh. Jesus came that I might have life more abundantly. And I sometimes think that if I knew what I know now, I would be in a better position. But God will bring you in when the time is right. We run a long time, but running is sometimes an experience we need to help others along the way, once we come to Christ.
O- Change into obedience. When he called me that day in New Orleans, I answered Yes to the call and tried him as my Savior. To love me in spite of all my wrong doing
O- Change into Overcomer. I am overcoming obstacles everyday and he still loves me. Never leave me alone, we talk and have the best conversation.
 D- Change into believing my dreams would come true; I am willing to delight myself into the word of God. I do this daily which has become a lifestyle.

So today I say to The Blood OF Christ "Thank You"!!!! For your grace and mercy, forgiveness, protection, guidance, friendship, peace, unfailing love, my Savior, your Savior.
Amen!!!!

Mission Questions:
(A) Why do you want more people in the Church?
(B) Are you a mission driver? Or position driver?
(C) Is more mission more money?
(D)Are you on a mission, what is your Mission